SNAILS & SLUGS

Written by Graham Meadows & Claire Vial

CONTENTS

DOMINIE PRESS
Pearson Learning Group

Red Trumpet Shell ▲

Black Slug ▶

2

ABOUT SNAILS AND SLUGS

Snails and slugs belong to a group of animals called gastropods. The word *gastropod* means "stomach-foot." They were given this name because they have a large, muscular foot. To scientists, a slug is simply a snail that has a very small shell, or no shell at all.

Snails and slugs are related to octopuses, mussels, and other shellfish.

Snails and slugs are found in most areas of the world and in a variety of **habitats**. Those most familiar to us live on land, mainly in moist areas. But the largest number of snails and slugs live in the sea. Others live in fresh water.

Giant African Land Snail ▶

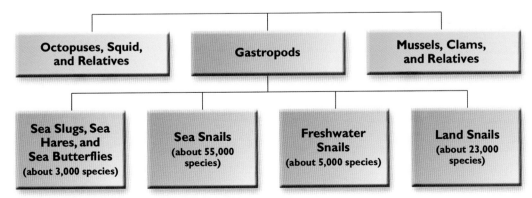

WHAT THEY LOOK LIKE

Snails and slugs have soft bodies. Most of those that live on land have two pairs of tentacles. They use their tentacles for feeling and smelling. They have eyes on the tips of one pair of tentacles.

Most snails have a shell made up of coils, called whorls. As a snail grows, it adds more whorls to its shell.

Many land slugs have a small, flat shell that is hidden under their skin. Many sea slugs have no shell at all.

Most snails and slugs have a rough "tongue," called a radula. The radula is covered with very small teeth. It acts as a sort of **rasp**, or file.

◀ **Tiger Slug**

▲ **Banded Wood Snails**

◀ **Common Garden Snail**

Clown Sea Slug ▲

SEA SLUGS

Sea slugs are found throughout the world, mainly in **tropical** waters. Some sea slugs live in shallow water, and some swim in the open ocean. Many are brightly colored to warn **predators** that they have a nasty taste or are poisonous.

Sea slugs range in size from less than one inch to twelve inches long. They either have a shell hidden under their skin, or they have no shell at all. Many of them have no tentacles. Many **species** of sea slugs have feathery gills, but some have none. Sea slugs can breathe through their skin.

Jason Sea Slug ▲

Some sea slugs feed on small animals such as sponges, sea anemones, corals, and fish eggs. Others feed on algae and seaweed.

7

SEA HARES AND SEA BUTTERFLIES

Sea hares and sea butterflies are types of sea slugs.

Sea hares are so named because they have tentacles that look like a rabbit's ears. They are found all around the world in **temperate** and tropical waters. They **survive** on a **diet** of algae.

Sea butterflies got their name because many of them have a pair of large, wing-like flaps that they use for swimming. Their bodies are almost totally **transparent**. They are found in all the world's oceans, even in **frigid** Arctic and Antarctic waters. They live mainly at or near the water's surface, feeding on plankton.

Sea slugs, sea hares, and sea butterflies are also called nudibranchs.

◀ Little Sea Hare

▼ Sea Butterfly

Black Nerita Snail (left), Hairy Trumpet Shell (right) ▲

SEA SNAILS

The group of animals known as sea snails includes limpets, whelks, winkles, cowries, abalones, and trumpet shells. Trumpet shells are also known as triton shells. Many of them have a special lid, called an operculum, on their foot. When the snail goes into its shell, the operculum seals the entrance. This helps to protect the snail from predators.

Some sea snails use their muscular foot to crawl around on rocks, sand, or vegetation. Others use it to **burrow** into the sand and move around underneath it. Many snails that burrow under the sand have pointed shells.

Many sea snails are **herbivores**, meaning they eat only plants. Others, such as the Arabic volute shell, are **carnivores**, meaning they eat other animals. Some carnivores, such as whelks, can drill through the shell of an oyster or clam.

Arabic Volute Shell ▶

11

FRESHWATER SNAILS

Freshwater snails are found all over the world. They live in many different habitats, such as ponds, lakes, streams, and rivers. Some freshwater snails even live in hot springs.

Some freshwater snails have gills for breathing. They can live at the bottom of ponds. Others have lungs for breathing. They must live on or near the water's surface.

Like sea snails, many freshwater snails have a special lid, called an operculum, on their foot. The operculum seals the entrance to the shell and helps to protect the snail from predators.

Freshwater snails, such as apple snails, mainly feed on algae. Some eat plants or the tiny animals that live on the plants.

◀ **Apple Snail**

◀ **Apple Snails**

Common ▶
Garden Snail

LAND SNAILS

▲ **Superb Land Snail**

Land snails are found almost everywhere in the world. They mainly live in damp, shady places, hiding or resting under leaves, logs, or stones. Most land snails live on the ground. But in forests, especially tropical forests, many of them live in trees.

Most land snails are active at night and on cloudy or damp days, because they need a moist **environment** to stop them from drying out. They do not like bright sunlight or hot, dry environments. However, some land snails can survive such conditions. For example, the California desert snail lives deep down inside rockslides.

All land snails have a lung for breathing.

Snails have special glands that produce slime underneath their muscular foot. The slime helps them move over rough or sharp objects, and to crawl on vertical surfaces.

Some land snails move by contracting and relaxing their muscular foot in a wave-like motion.

Some land snails are herbivores. Others are **omnivores**. They eat both plants and animals. Still others are carnivores. They eat animals such as earthworms, insects, and other snails.

The giant African land snail can grow to eight inches or more in length.

▼ **Giant African Land Snail**

▲ **Common Garden Snail**

▲ Common Garden Snail

THE LAND SNAIL'S LIFE CYCLE

The land snail's **life cycle** begins when small eggs are laid about two weeks after **mating** has occurred. The eggs are laid singly or in groups under stones, logs, or fallen leaves. After a few weeks the eggs hatch into tiny snails that have a soft, transparent shell.

Land snails protect themselves during winter and dry periods. They hide under rocks, wood, or leaves, and use a special fluid to seal the opening of their shell.

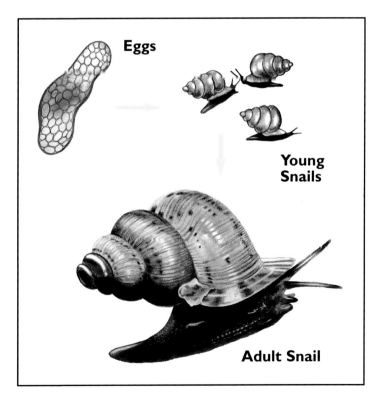

Eggs

Young Snails

Adult Snail

Some land snails have both male and female sexual organs.

LAND SLUGS

Some land slugs have a small shell that is hidden under their skin. Others have no shell at all. Most land slugs have two pairs of tentacles. All of them have a lung for breathing. Like snails, slugs have special glands that produce slime underneath their muscular foot.

Most land slugs are herbivores. Tiger slugs, also known as leopard slugs, are omnivores. They eat plants, but they also catch and eat other slugs. Some slugs, such as leafveined slugs, climb trees to search for food.

Leafveined Slug ▼

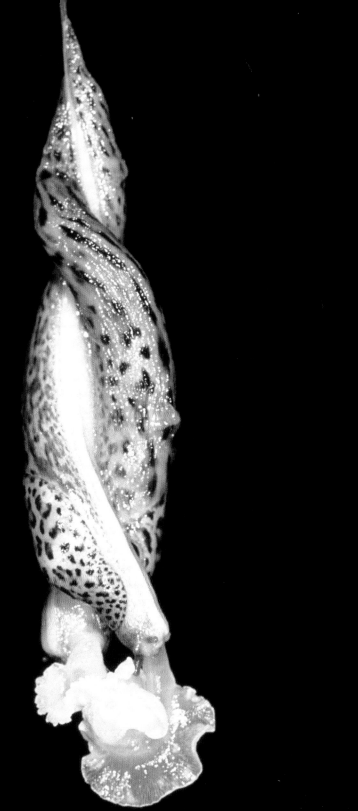

◀ Tiger Slugs Mating

SNAILS AND SLUGS, AND THEIR IMPORTANCE TO HUMANS

How They Are Useful

- Snails and slugs are an important part of the **food chain**. They eat plants, and in turn are eaten by animals such as frogs and birds.

- Humans also eat some types of snails, such as periwinkles and abalones.

- In France, land snails, which are called escargots, are specially grown for people to eat.

Limpkin Eating a Snail ▶

Tiger Slugs Eating Lettuce ▲

How They Are Harmful

- Snails and slugs can cause a lot of damage to crops. They can also be pests in gardens and greenhouses.

- Some snails and slugs carry **parasites** that can cause diseases in animals and humans.

GLOSSARY

burrow: To dig into something

carnivores: Animals that eat other animals

diet: The food that an animal or a person usually eats

environment: Surroundings; the setting where animals or people live

food chain: A term used to describe how all living things, predators and prey, feed on other living things in order to survive

frigid: Very, very cold

habitats: The places where animals and plants live and grow

herbivores: Animals that eat plants

life cycle: The stages, or phases, of an animal's development

mating: Joining with another animal in order to produce offspring

omnivores: Animals that eat both plants and other animals

parasites: Animals that live on other animals and use them to survive

predators: Animals that hunt, catch, and eat other animals

rasp: A type of file; a tool used for scraping or smoothing a surface

species: Types of animals that have some physical characteristics in common

survive: To stay alive and thrive

temperate: Land areas or bodies of water with a mild temperature and moderate climate

transparent: Easy to see through; allowing light to pass through

tropical: Areas that are very warm throughout the year

INDEX

Made in the USA
Coppell, TX
15 August 2020

33409743R00017